The Lotto and your Dreams Handbook

Introduction

As the first book MY DREAM MY KEY explains the methods used for converting your dreams into numbers, by using the Fa-Fi system, I strongly recommend that you get familiar with the terms of the book so that you can easily refer to this handbook. However, you can still learn dreams conversion the Fa-Fi way just by reading this book, but without the first book, it will take you some time to comprehend what Fa-Fi is and how it converts dreams into numbers.

You can buy it from the following major sites.

- Smashwords.com and associates.

- Amazon.com and associates.

- Lulu.com and associates.

- TheContentBazaar.com and associates.

- EBookbay.com and associates.

And a number of ClickBank affiliates worldwide. It is not hard to find.

Let's Begin by showing you Examples of Dreams and Conversions

Let's assume this dream as your own, shall we? Then later, we show you how to convert dreams, step by step.

Check the numbers from the New Jersey –Pick Six above, dated 3 Nov 2011.

38	New Jersey - Pick Six	3 Nov 2011	4,11,28,38,42,46 Payout

You park your Car (11), and get to the subway to take a Train (46 also 10) to work. To your Surprise (28), a Gentleman (42 also 6) approaches you and ask for a 10 Dollars (38 also 2), you tell him that he is asking for a Fortune (4) but you give him anyway.

Do you see all the symbols and images from the dream? 4, 11, 28,38,42,46 are the corresponding numbers, which in this case, are the winning numbers. This could have been your chance to win.

All the winning numbers are derived from the conversion. All you need to know is what symbol is attached to what number. Let's visit more results from different countries.

🇨🇦

14	Canada - Western 6/49	5 Nov 2011	1,4,14,17,26,29 37 Payout

Dream:

"…you attend a Teary (29) Funeral (26), of an Old Woman (14) who has left her King Son (1 also 37) and her Queen (17) daughter in law a Fortune (4). "

11	Canada - Lotto 649	5 Nov 2011	14,18,22,34,36,43 3 Payout

Dream:

"…you see an Old Woman (14), in the Rain (18) going through the Dirt (34), holding a Cigar (36) in one hand a Big Stick (43 also 7). Frogs (3) jumping next to the old woman's bare feet as she saved her Shoes (22).from the wet weather"

8	Brazil – Mega-Sena	5 Nov 2011	1,6,8,10,25,27 Payout

Brazil here we go:

"You dream of your cousin who is a wanted by Cops (27) because he robbed a Mansion (25). You are so furious that you call him a Cow (6). However, you take him to a Train (10) station to take refuge by your cousin out of town. You leave to buy some ticket only to come back to find him Drunk (8) and Bloody (1)"

7	Belgium – Lotto	5 Nov 2011	4,14,21,25,33,42 39 Payout

DREAM:

"Your Old Mother (14) is telling you of your Late Father's (4) secrets of fathering some Boys (33). You tell her that your father was such a Gentleman (42 also 6) and he worked hard to provide her with a Big House (25). She also tells you that your father died of a stab wound {a Knife} (21) and not by an Accident (39 also 3) and you cry frantically" Scary!!!

6	Austria – Lotto	2 Nov 2011	4,23,31,32,36,45 28 Payout

Austrian Dreamer:

"Your Doctor (23) charges you a Fortune (4) for your Child (45 also 9) health, and you decide to take it up with him. You then take it to the Bishop (31) but you are Surprised (28) as he asks you for more Paper Money (32). You tell him that he is such a Dick (36) and you walk out."

4	Australia – Saturday Lotto	5 Nov 2011	2,6,12,18,44,45	28,32 Payout

G'Day Mate…

"You consoling a Gentleman (6) who just found out that his Pregnant (44 also 8) wife is Dead (12), while giving birth to their Baby (45 also 9). You get Surprised (28) as he mentions the Money (2) he is going to get and that he says he is going to blow it on Gold (32) stock. He will only give his mother in law some Small change (18)"

3	Australia – Powerball Lotto	3 Nov 2011	2,5,18,22,44	9 Payout

Let's check the Power-Ball. Here's your Dream…

"You are Drunk (8) and looking to hitch-hike a lift in the Rain (18), and you try to run but lose your Shoe (22). You finally decide to take a cab and yet you have no Money (2). Then you meet up with some Muscular Guy (5) and you walk with him home under the Moonlight (9)"

It's a complicated dream like any other but a dream nonetheless. Have you noticed how dreams are?

2	Australia – Oz Lotto	1 Nov 2011	5,12,17,23,25,31,44	13,19 Payout

Dream:

"A Queen (12) who is highly regarded as a Lady (17) taking her pet Tiger (5) for a walk around the Castle (25) and she constantly touches her Crown (23). She reaches for her Lipstick (31) when she sees a Chinese (44 also 8) gardener to entice him. She touches her tigers Tail (13) as she passes by. She then sits to take a Smoke (19)."

63	Wisconsin – Megabucks	5 Nov 2011	2,18,33,45,46,48 Payout

Dream:

It is Easter morning and you have your Boys (33) asking you for Money (2) to buy some chocolate Eggs (46 also 10). You search for some loose Coins (18) but you can't find any. You then ask them to join you by the Fire (48 also 12) where you have prepared them a lovely Dish (45 also 9)

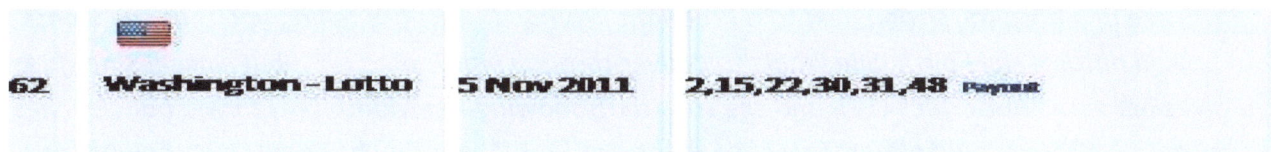

62	Washington – Lotto	5 Nov 2011	2,15,22,30,31,48 Payout

Dream:

You have this nightmare about a woman with a glossy Lipstick (31), who your husband spend Money on (2) and buy her Shoes (22). You later run into her and you call her a Slut (15) and hold her by the Throat (30). You throw her into a Fire (12). Holy Toledo!

61	Vermont – Megabucks Plus	5 Nov 2011	9,11,20,21,25 2 Payout

Dream:

You dream of spending Money (2) on this Mansion (25) because you are expecting a Baby (9). You also want to sell your Car (11) and your Music (20) collection. You smile at that thought so much your Teeth (21) are showing.

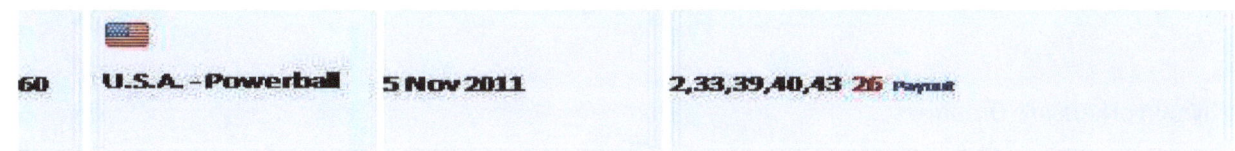

60	U.S.A. – Powerball	5 Nov 2011	2,33,39,40,43 26 Payout

You are attending a Funeral (26) of A Crooked (43 also 7) Driver Pilot (2) who died (40 also 4) from an Airplane (33) Accident (39 also 3).

16	Connecticut – Classic Lotto	4 Nov 2011	4,6,7,8,15,17 Payout

The Dream and Numbers:

You see a Gentleman (6) who has quite a fortune (4) and somehow, married a crooked (7) Lady (17), who always behaves like a whore (15) when drunk (8).

Consider this one for fun…

…You are in a hospital, sitting next to a Pregnant Woman (8), who is telling you that she wants to have a natural child birth. She wants to deliver through her Vagina (35), but since it's her first, it gives her some Butterflies (18), and she says that, showing her Mouth (24) to you but clenches her Teeth (21). You could almost feel her Excitement (31). And later she comes out showing you her baby (27).

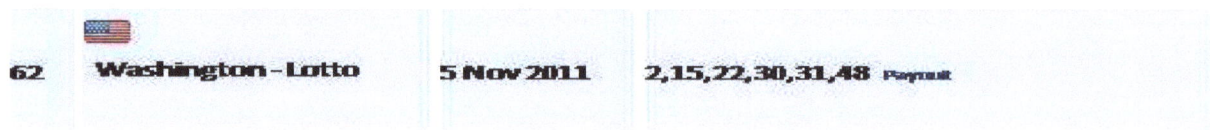

62	Washington – Lotto	5 Nov 2011	2,15,22,30,31,48 Payout

Dream:

In a Forest (30) nearby, there's a Fire (12). You see a Monkey (2) riding on a White Horse (15) back, with a flipping of a Horseshoe (31) flying from the horse's left foot (hoof) (22) as it sprints near you.

Can you see the flow of authentic events in this dream? Amazing isn't it?

40	New York – Sweet Million Lotto	3 Nov 2011	2,5,10,16,27,30 Payout

New Yorkers are Dreamers….

You are in a cab, and you talking to an Indian (30) Driver (2), when a Cop (27), stops a cab for speeding. There is an Argument (5) between the two and then they grab each other by their Clothes (16). You abandon the cab and decide to catch a Train (10).

Realistic isn't it? It's like you had this dream yesterday.

The Dream:

You are outside your riverside Mansion (25) and you are out fishing (21). Your luck increases and you catch this Big Fish (49 also 13). You get into your Car (47 also 11) and drive to your mom's and on the driveway, you get a warm welcome from you Little Niece (19) who takes you in the house. Your first sight is this warm glowing Fire (12) in the grand hall.

| 59 | U.S.A. - Mega Millions | 4 Nov 2011 | 26,30,32,33,44 1 Payout |

Mega Dreams for Mega Millions…

You are attending a Funeral (26) where a Fat (44 also 8) Priest (30) is preaching. Suddenly a very Drunk (8) Ill-mannered wife (32) starts to sob uncontrollably, saying her King (1) is dead. This had some Young Boy (33) giggling.

| 47 | South Africa – Powerball | 8 Nov 2011 | 8,10,11,15,45 20 Payout |

…you go to the fridge and open it, and then you take out some Pork (8) Ribs (11) out and put them on a Dish (45 also 9). You try to pull a piece to taste, but decide to use a Small Knife (15). Then you take some Eggs (10) and boil them. You wipe the fat from the ribs with your Handkerchief (20)."

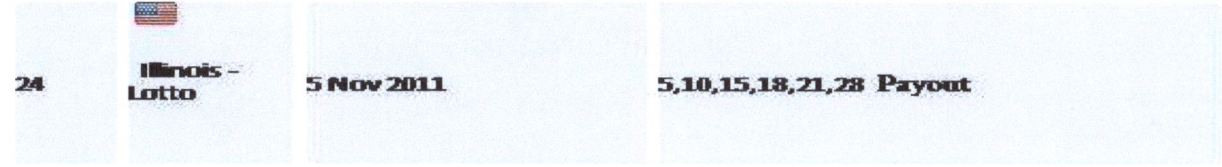

| 24 | Illinois – Lotto | 5 Nov 2011 | 5,10,15,18,21,28 Payout |

You dream you are in Rainy weather (18) fishing (21: a fisherman). You are surprised (28) to catch a Tiger (5) shark. When you cut open it with a small knife (15), you see it had some Eggs (10) in its body.

Though a shark doesn't lay eggs, but in dreams, anything goes. Hence they are called dreams.

40	New York – Sweet Million Lotto	7 Nov 2011	2,6,17,23,35,37 Payout

…you are lured by the charm of this Gentleman (6) and Lady (17) who promises you Money (2). They invite you to their House (23) and you go with a smile on your face. On arrival, you notice the house is huge but very Hollow (35). You notice there's Blood (01) on the floor and you run out of the house.

The Process

Let's map the process for you and you will begin to understand how to convert.

Step by Step Mentoring

- ### Number Chart

This is a chart which is more like previous draws chart, where you write all the numbers drawn by date and time. This helps you to check what numbers are HOT under What Parity Rule in the Lotto system your country is using. Change the numbers back to their natural form, i.e. from number 1 to number 36. Note that all shaded areas are equal either 35 or 36 when added together.

Power- Ball or Lotto Results (In their Natural Form)

Ball 1	Ball 2	Ball 3	Ball 4	Ball 5	Ball 6
6	2	3	16	23	9
2	32	12	8	15	13
20	15	21	35	31	5
24	3	8	7	10	8
2	36	33	4	8	4
26	4	6	10	8	4
28	24	35	11	21	17
22	4	1	8	7	18
24	27	25	22	5	5
8	23	31	10	2	8
3	2	28	2	4	20
5	11	8	17	28	20
4	36	10	23	18	4
30	1	5	4	2	3
15	9	34	7	25	1
2	19	4	5	1	15
10	3	20	36	18	13
20	4	31	17	22	13
28	5	19	21	14	11
21	3	16	10	22	9
8	5	2	3	7	16

The Wheel of Fortune (The most important part of this book)

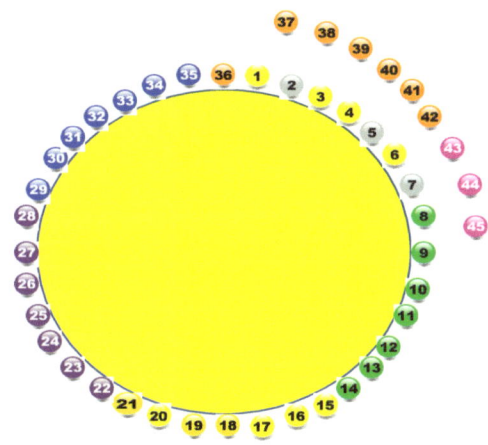

Remember that the Wheel has an extension of numbers from 37 to whatever number as per your country's lotto system.

Refer to MY DREAM MY KEY *Book.*

Once you have considered the numbers drawn from the last twelve draws, remove all the numbers, noting Hot numbers as you go along. Your Wheel of Fortune will look something like this bearing very few numbers.

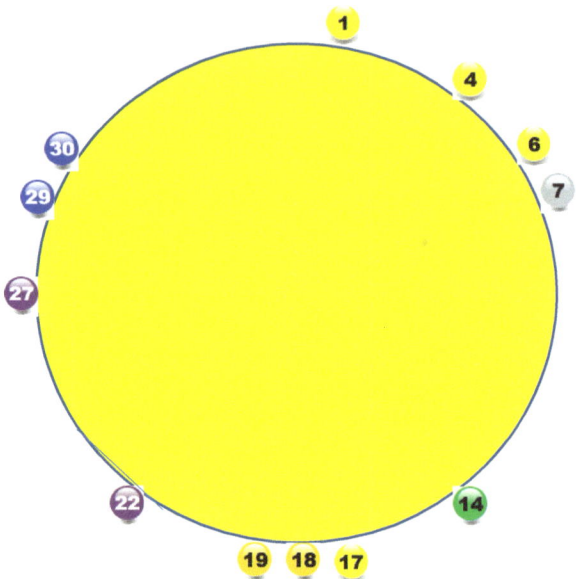

- ## Dream Journal

I assume you have kept your dream journal for some time now. If you haven't, it is not too late, you can start with the dreams you have noted recently and continue from there. The key issue here is how you convert these dream symbols into numbers. You will need to consult with the images or objects. Consider this dream example and see how it is plotted using dream conversion methods.

You are in a hospital where a Chinese Nurse, is bringing you a piece of Steak. Instead you find yourself being fondled and some Eggs which you take from the plate fall. The good nurse takes out a Gun. She pulls the trigger but the bullet accidentally hits a passerby.

- ## Dream Conversion

Now that you have pointed out the key images, objects or symbols in your dream, you must visit the dreams symbols and their corresponding numbers for easy conversion. This should be straight forward for you. Here is how you should do it.

Chinese **(12)** *Nurse* **(14),**

Steak **(34).**

Eggs **(10)**

Gun **(36),**

Accident **(3),**

Move on to the next phase

- ## Parity Rule

This chart below shows the extension table and parity. The Rule is explained thoroughly in MY DREAM MY KEY Book.

A	B	A2	B2
1	36	37	
2	29	38	
3	8	39	44
4	15	40	
4	35	40	
5	19	41	
6	33	42	
7	13	43	49
9	17	45	
10	23	46	
11	26	47	
12	34	48	
14	32	Etc	
16	35	Etc	
18	31	Etc	
20	25	Etc	
21	24	Etc	
22	27	Etc	
26	30	Etc	
28	30	Etc	

- ## Law of 36

12	14	34	3	10	+36

Where your dream is concerned, this is how your numbers will show on the law of 36 charts or table.

Can you see in their natural form, that 10+12+14=36? Then this shows you that you are on the right track, as far as the Fa-Fi system is concerned.

- Selection

Plot your numbers using the above steps should your dream have more than six symbols. In fact you still need to pair your numbers using the HOT and COLD method. Remember in the beginning you had a Wheel of Fortune which you removed the previously drawn numbers.

Now check your numbers and the HOT numbers, as your dream had unfolded, and plot your selection. You will need to plot more than one row of numbers for better chances of winning.

- Revisit Parity Rule

This you need to do because you have selected more than one row or bet and you need to ascertain all the steps are followed.

Remember that Parity Rules are from Parity 1-36 to Parity 26-28-30.

- Place your Final Numbers

Though the book does not guarantee you a definite win, in time, you will use your money sparingly when you choose your numbers that are given to you by the POWER of THE UNIVERSE through your dreams. Make sure you consider the first *"Gut Feel'* selection first.

The Symbols and Numbers

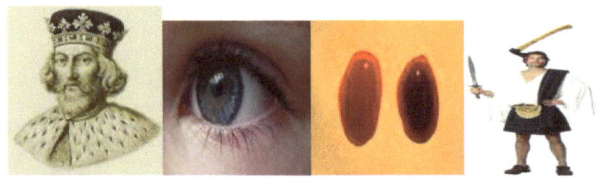

...

- *King*
- *Left Eye*
- *Blood*
- *Whiteman*

36

- *Cigar*
- *Gun*
- *Any Oblong Shaped Object*
- *Penis*

2

- *Monkey*
- *Money*
- *Jockey*
- *Blackman*
- *Driver*

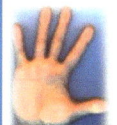

29

- *Small Water*
- *Tears*
- *Right Hand*
- *Milk*
- *Big Knife*

3

- **Big Water**
- **Accident**
- **Frog**
- **Sex**

   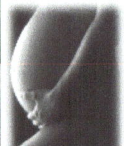 

8

- **Pig**
- **Drunkard**
- **Stout Person**
- **Pregnant Person**
- **Chinese**

4

- **Dead Man**
- **Bed**
- **Bee**
- **Turkey**
- **Fortune**

  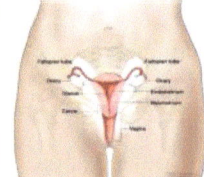

- *Big Hole*
- *Grave*
- *Hollow Things*
- *Vagina*

15

- *Prostitute (or someone behaving as such)*
- *White Horse*
- *Small Knife*

16

- *Clothes*
- *Dove*
- *Animal Ears*
- *Ship*
- *Small House*
- *Flag*
- *Money*

- *Tiger (not in the Woods)*
- *Fight*
- *Muscular Or Strong Man*

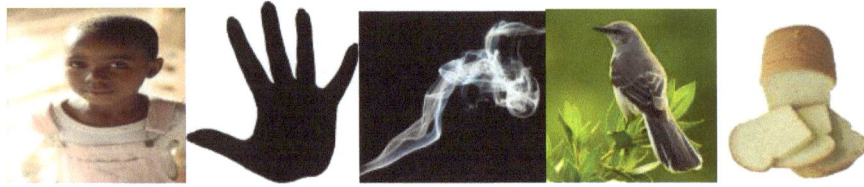

- *Young Girl/s*
- *Left Hand*
- *Smoke*
- *Bird*
- *Bread*

- *Cow*
- *Gentleman*

- *Young Boy/s*
- *Toys*
- *Clouds*
- *Plane*
- *Spider*

- *Con-Man*
- *Lion*
- *Big Stick*
- *Chicken*

- *Big Fish*
- *Ghost*
- *Tail*

- *Moon*
- *Owl*
- *Hat*
- *Baby*
- *Lamp*
- *Dish*
- *Pumpkin*

- *Diamond/s*
- *Lady*
- *Queen*
- *White Woman*

- *Egg/s*
- *Ball*
- *Train*
- *Round Object*

   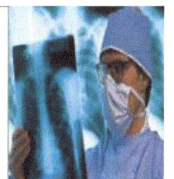

- *House*
- *Crown*
- *Hair*
- *Head*
- *Doctor*

 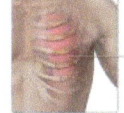  

- *Chicken Feet*
- *Car*
- *Ribs*

- *Funeral*
- *Bees*
- *Bush*
- *Mad Person*

- **Dead Woman**
- **Chinese**
- **Queen**
- **Fire**

- *Paper Money (Notes)*
- *Gold nuggets or Bar*
- *Snake*
- *Ill-mannered Woman*

- *Old Woman*
- *Nurse*
- *Detective*

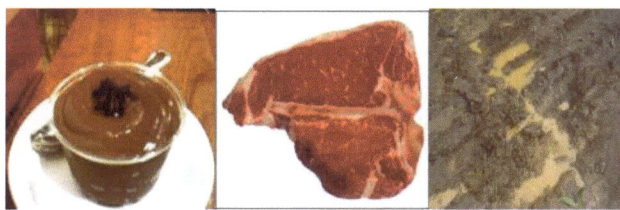

- *Faeces or Defecation*
- *Dirty Objects*
- *Pudding*
- *Mud*
- *Meat*

- *Coins (or loose change)*
- *Right Eye*
- *Chain*
- *Belt*
- *Rain*
- *Butterfly*

- *Fire*
- *Feather*
- *Lipstick*

- *Horse Shoe*
- *Bishop*
- *Excitement*

20

- *Cat*
- *Music*
- *Paymaster*
- *Driver*
- *Nude Woman*
- *Handkerchief*

25

- *Big House*
- *Boxer*

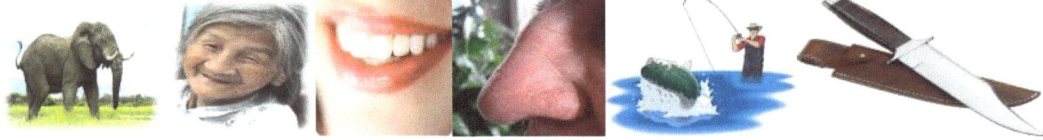

21

- *Elephant*
- *Old Woman*

- *Teeth*
- *Nose*
- *Fisherman*
- *Knife*

- *Mouth*
- *Purse*
- *Wild Cat.*

     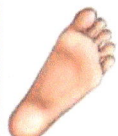 

- *Ship*
- *Shoes*
- *Car*
- *Bed*
- *Cats*
- *Left Foot*

  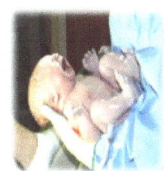  

- *Dog*
- *Policeman*
- *Newborn*
- *Medicine*
- *Sad news*

 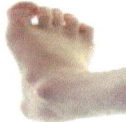   

- *Small Fish*
- *Right foot*
- *Shoes*
- *Turf*
- *Surprise*
- *Child*

- *Chicken (Live one)*
- *Priest*
- *Sun*
- *Forest*
- *Throat*
- *Indian*

Power-Ball's Wheel of Fortune

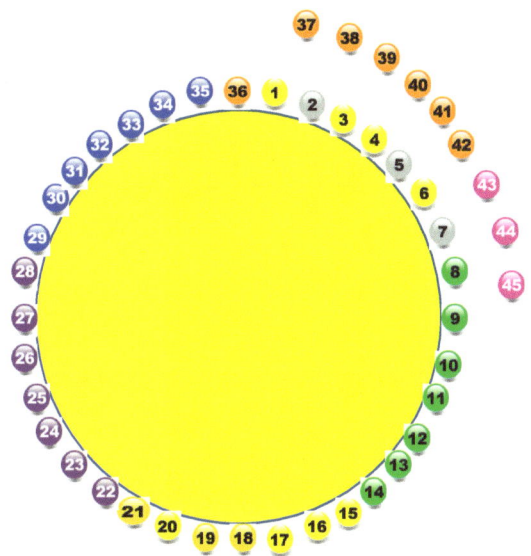

Table of Extensions

1	37	Power-Ball and Lotto
2	38	Power-Ball and Lotto
3	39	Power-Ball and Lotto
4	40	Power- Ball and Lotto
5	41	Power-Ball and Lotto
6	42	Power-Ball and Lotto
7	43	Power-Ball and Lotto
8	44	Power-Ball and Lotto
9	45	Power-Ball and Lotto
10	46	Lotto
11	47	Lotto
12	48	Lotto
13	49	Lotto

Note: The Table can go on and on until the cycle repeat itself. Your Country may use a system of 6/72.

The dreams are all restricted to 36, which mean if you dream of a King, you will either choose 1 or 37.

Points to Ponder

- Dreams Symbols don't change
- Parity Laws don't change
- Law of 36 doesn't change
- *Some countries go up to 80 Number System but the numbers still revolve around the Initial Universal Law of 360 degrees or 36 Number System.*

The Parity Law 2 and 29

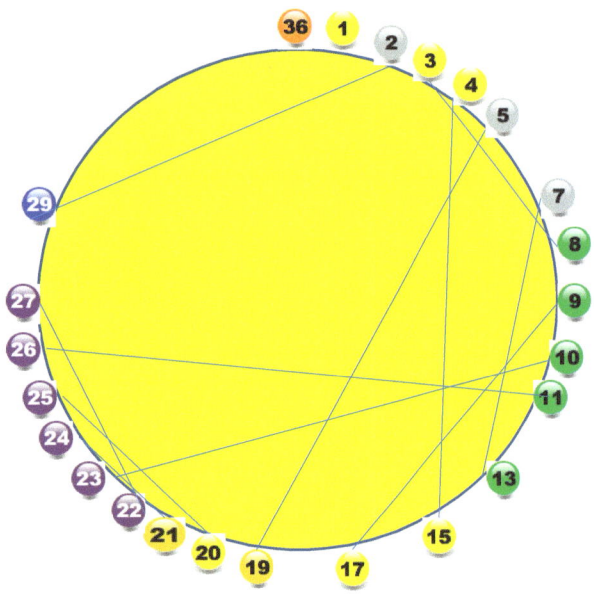

The Numbers restricted to share the spotlight are:

6, 33,

12, 32,

14, 34,

16, 35,

 18, 31,

28, 30 and note that there is no line crossing a 2 and 29 *connecting line*

The Parity Law 3 and 8

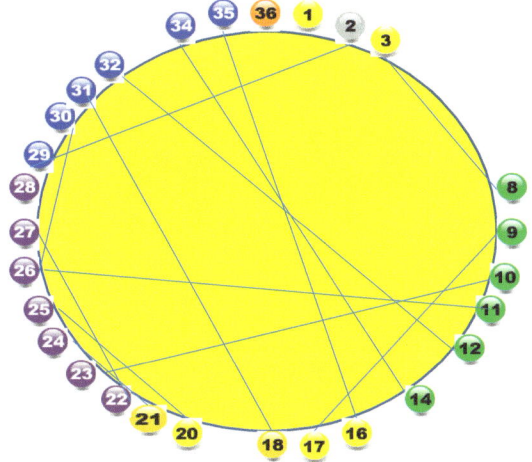

Restrictions are to:

4, 15

5, 19

6, 33

7, 13

And note that there is no line that crosses the 3 and 8 *connecting line*

The Parity Law 4 and 15

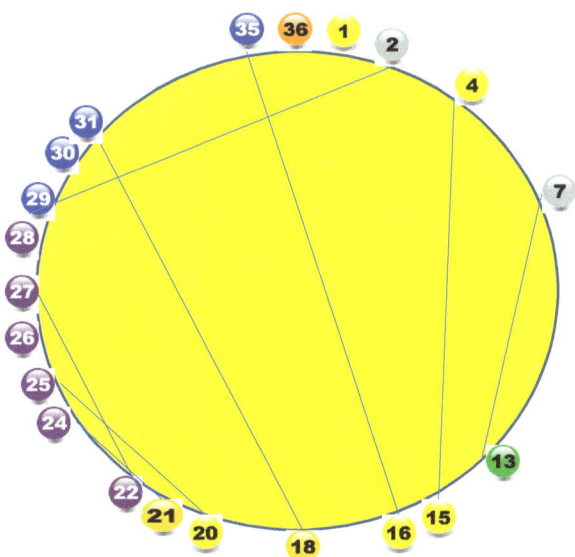

Restrictions:

3, 8

5, 19

6, 33

9, 17

10, 23

11

12, 32 and 14, 34 and note there's no line that crosses the 4 and 15 *connecting line*

The Parity Law 4 and 35

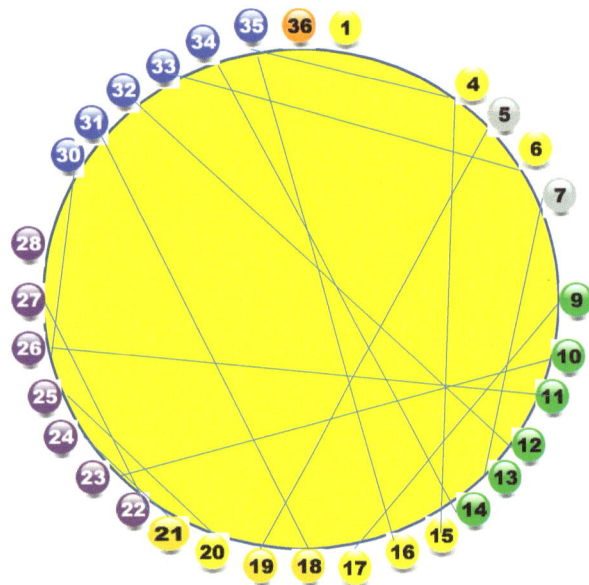

Restrictions:

3, 8

2, 29

And note there's no line that crosses the 4 and 35 *connecting line*

The Parity Law 5 and 19

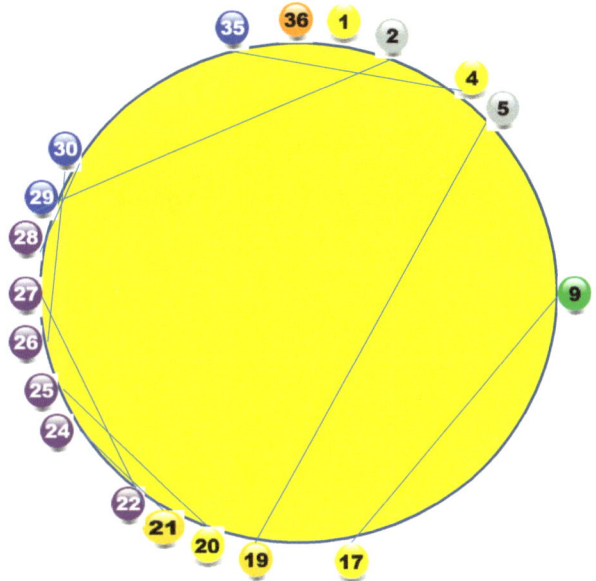

Restrictions:

3, 8

6, 33

7, 13

10, 23

11, 15, 12, 32,

14, 34, 18, 31 and note: no line that crosses 5 and 19 *connecting line*

The Parity Law 6 and 33

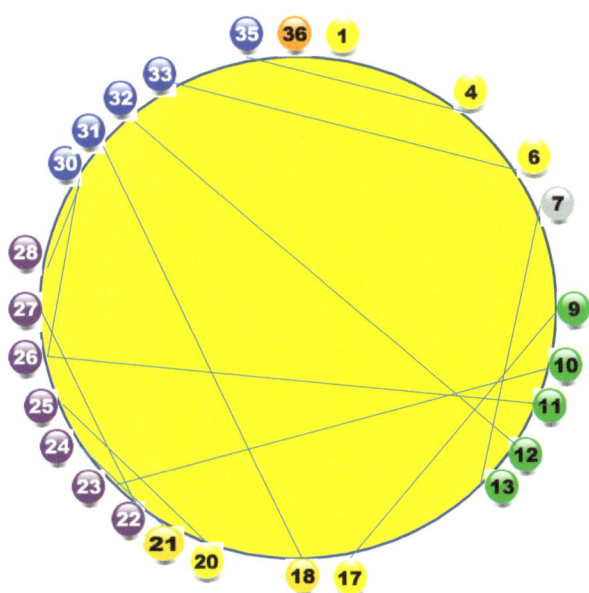

Restrictions:

2, 29

3, 8

5, 19

14, 34

15

16 and note that there's no line that crosses the 6 and 33 *connecting line*

The Parity Law 7 and 13

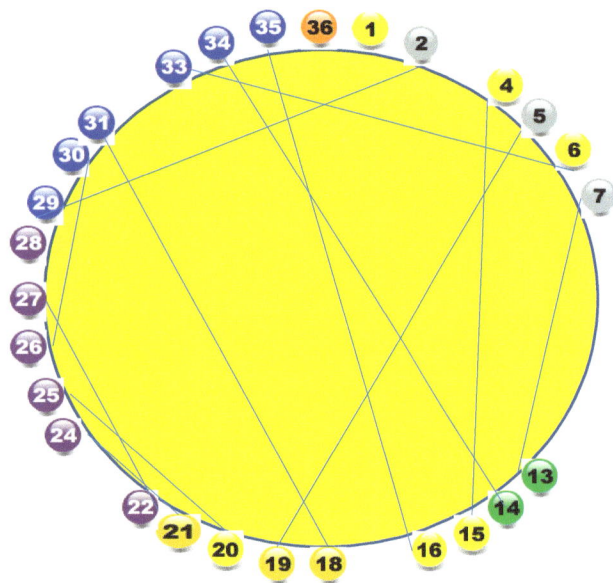

Restrictions:

3, 8

9, 17

10, 23

11

12, 32

And note that there's no line that crosses the 7 and 13 *connecting line*

The Parity Law 9 and 17

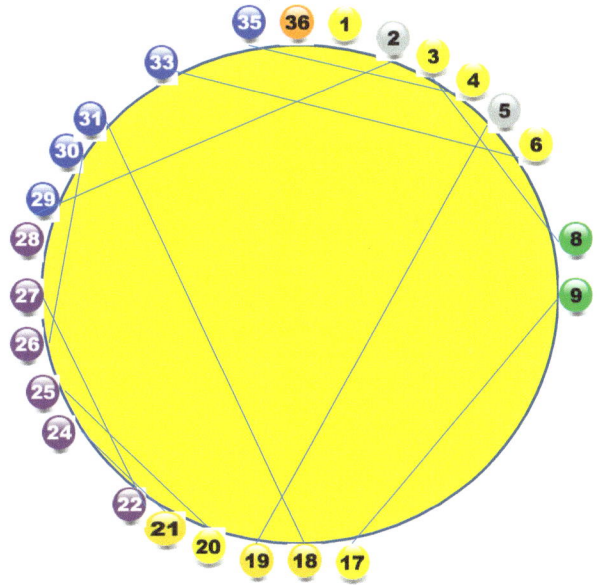

Restrictions:

7, 13

10, 23

11

12, 32

14, 34

15, 16, and note that there's no line that crosses the 9 and 17 *connecting line*

The Parity Law 10 and 23

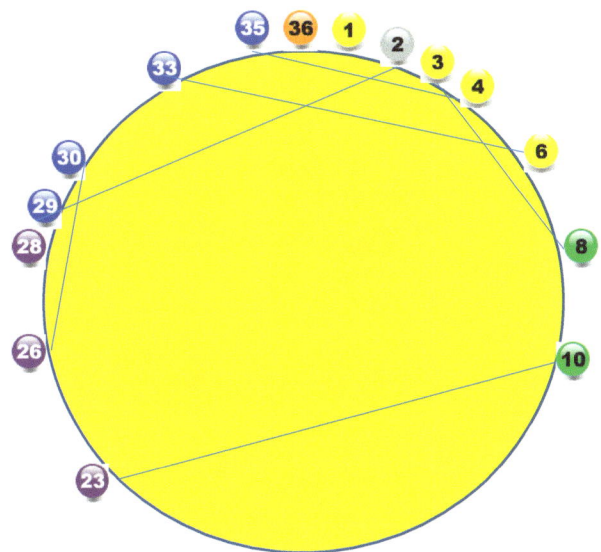

Restrictions:

5, 19

7, 13

9, 17

11, 26

12, 32

14, 34

16,

18, 31,

20, 25, 21, 24, 22, 27 and note there's no line that crosses the 10 and 23 *connecting line*

The Parity Law 11 and 26

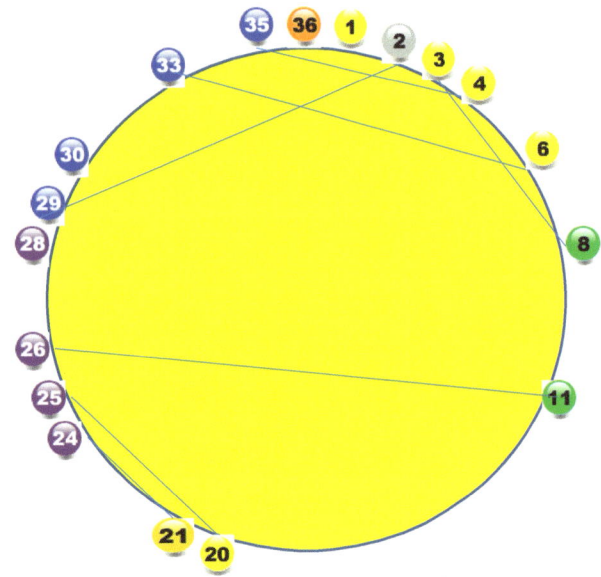

Restrictions:

5, 19

7, 13

9, 17

10, 23

12, 32,

14, 34, 16,

 18, 31,

22, 27 and note that there's no line that crosses the 11 and 26 *connecting line*

The Parity Law 12 and 32

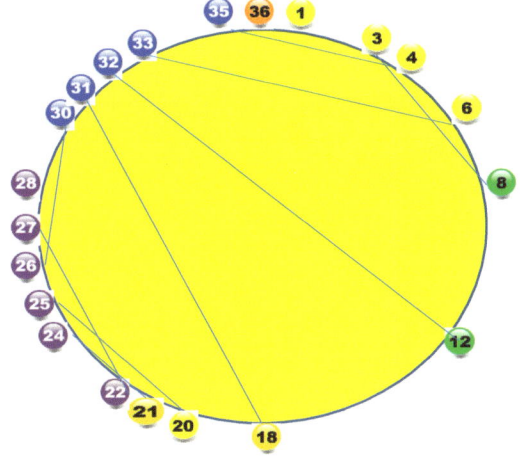

Restrictions:

2, 29

5, 19

7, 13

9, 17

10, 23

11, 14, 34, 16, and note that there's no line that crosses the 12 and 32 *connecting line*

The Parity Law 14 and 34

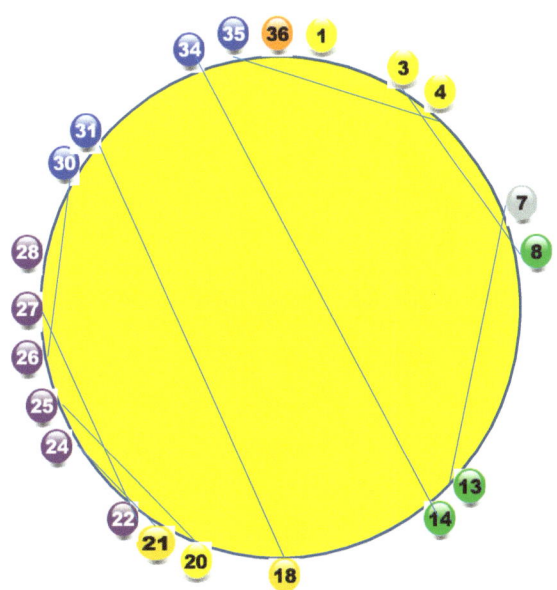

Restrictions:

2, 29

5, 19

6, 33

9, 17

10, 23

11

12, 32, 15, 16, and note that there's no line that crosses the 14 and 34 *connecting line*

The Parity Law 16 and 35

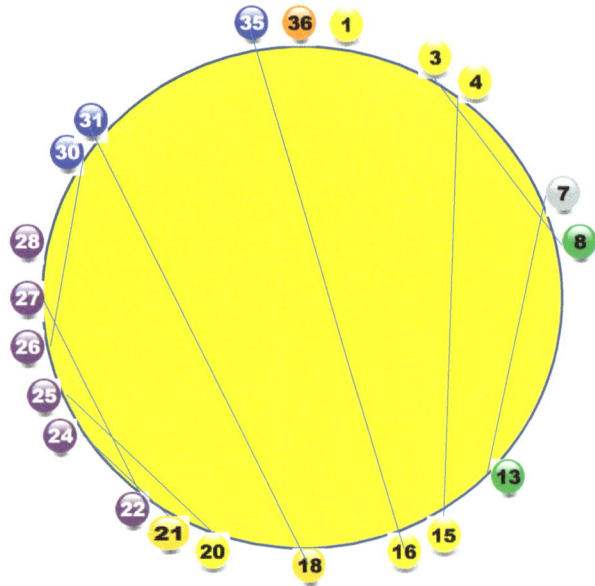

Restrictions:

5, 19

6, 33

9, 17

10, 23

11

12, 32

14, 34, and note that there's no line that crosses the 16 and 35 *connecting line*

The Parity Law 18 and 31

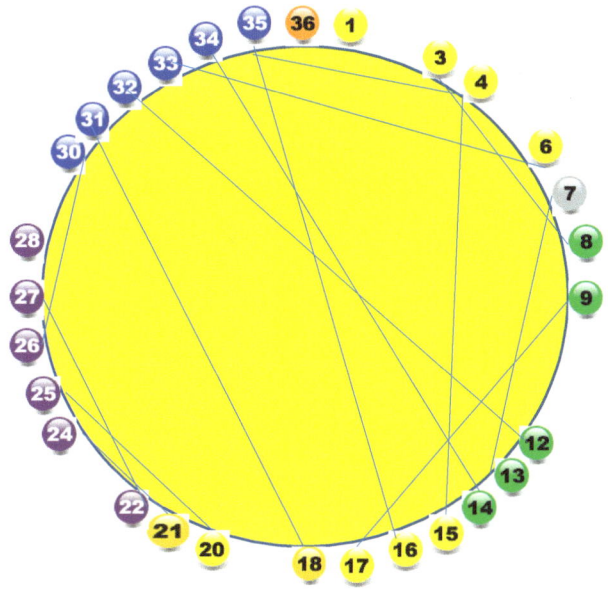

Restrictions:

2, 29

5, 19

10, 23

11

And note that there's no line that crosses the 18 and 31 *connecting line*

The Parity Law 20 and 25 & 21 and 24

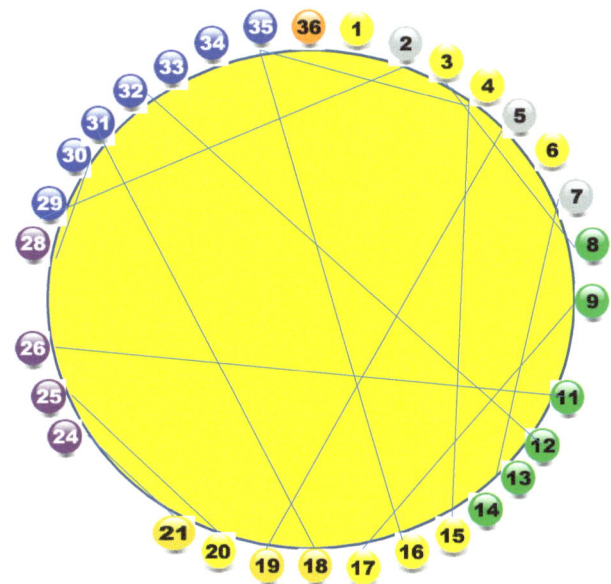

Restrictions;

22, 27

And note that there's no line that crosses the 20 and 25, 21 and 24 *connecting line*

The Parity Law 22 and 27

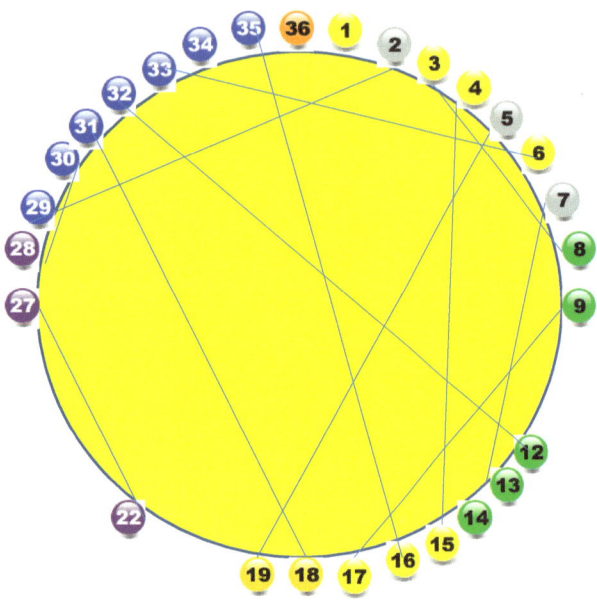

Restrictions:

10, 23

11, 26

20, 25

21, 24

And note that there's no line that crosses the 22 and 27 *connecting line*

The Parity Law 26, 28 and 30

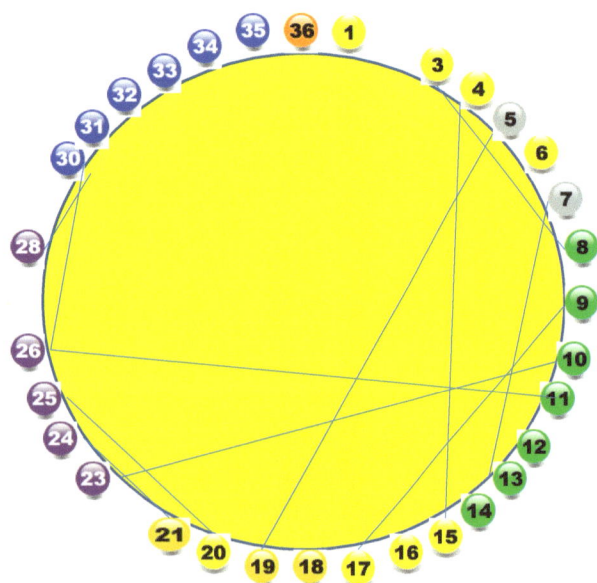

Restrictions:

2, 29

22, 27

The Law of  in Action!

Let's see…

You park your Car (11), and get to the subway to take a Train (46 also 10) to work. To your Surprise (28), a Gentleman (42 also 6) approaches you and ask for a 10 Dollars (38 also 2), you tell him that he is asking for a Fortune (4) but you give him anyway.

Law of 36

4   11   28   38   42   46

38, 28 and 42 gives you 36. You should know by now that 38 is also 2, and 42 is 6.

Dream:

"…you attend a Teary (29) Funeral (26), of an Old Woman (14) who has left her King son (1 also 37) and her Queen (17) daughter in law a Fortune (4).

Law Of 36

1   4   14   17   26   29   37

"…you see an Old Woman (14), in the Rain (18) going through the Dirt (34), holding a Cigar (36) in one hand a Big Stick (43 also 7). Frogs (3) jumping next to the old woman's bare feet as she saved her Shoes (22)."

Law Of 36

14   18   22   34   36   43   3

14, 18 and 3 = 35

Dream:

"You dream of your cousin who is a wanted by Cops (27) because he robbed a Mansion (25). You are so furious that you call him a Cow (6). However, you take him to a Train (10) station. You leave to buy some ticket only to come back to find him Drunk (8) and Bloody (1)

Law of 36

1	6	8	10	25	27

1 …8…27…=36

DREAM:

"Your old Mother (14) is telling you of your Late Father's (4) secrets of fathering some Boys (33). You tell her that your father was such a Gentleman (42 also 6) and he worked hard to provide her with a Big House (25). She also tell you that your father died of a stab wound {a Knife} (21) and not by an Accident (39 also 3) and you cry frantically" Scary!!!

Law of 36

4	14	21	25	33	42	39

14 and 21=35   please look for some combinations here.

Dream:

"Your Doctor (23) charges you a Fortune (4) for your Child (45 also 9) health, and you decide to take it up with him. You then take it to the Bishop (31) but you are Surprised (28) as he asks you for more Paper Money (32). You tell him that he is such a Dick (36) and you walk out."

Law Of 36

4	23	31	32	36	45	28

4 and 32 is 36   31 and 4 is 35   23 and 9 and 4 is 36

"You consoling a Gentleman (6) who just found out that his Pregnant (44 also 8) wife is Dead (12), while giving birth to their Baby (45 also 9). You get Surprised (28) as he mentions the Money (2) he is going to get and that he says he is going to blow on Gold (32) stock. He will only give his mother in law some Small change (18)"

Law of 36

2	6	12	18	44	45	28	32

2…6…18 and 45 gives you 35. What is 45 again? You are right, it is 9.

Let's check the Power-Ball. Here's your Dream…

"You are Drunk (8) and looking for a lift in the Rain (18), you try to run but lose your Shoe (22). You finally decide to take a cab but you have no Money (2). Then you meet up with a Muscular Guy (5) and you walk with him home under the Moonlight (9)"

It's a complicated dream like any other but the dream nonetheless.

Law of 36

2   5   18   22   44   9

35 is what you get right?

Dream:

"A Queen (12) Lady (17) taking her pet Tiger (5) for a walk around the Castle (25), and she constantly touches her Crown (23). She reaches for her Lipstick (31) when she sees a Chinese (44 also 8) gardener to entice him. She touches her tigers Tail (13) as she passes by. She sits to take a Smoke (19)."

Law of 36

5   12   17   23   31   44   13   19

5, 23, 44 is 36.

Dream:

You have your Boys (33) asking you for Money (2) to buy some chocolate Eggs (46 also 10). You search for some Coins (18) but you can't find any. You ask them to join you by the Fire (48 also 12) where you have prepared them a lovely Dish (45 also 9)

Law of 36

2   18   33   45   46   48

2 + 33 is 35...easy way out huh.

Dream:

You have this nightmare about this woman with a glossy Lipstick (31), who your husband spend Money (2) and buy her Shoes (22). You later run into her and you call her a Slut (15) and hold her by the Throat (30). You throw her into a Fire (12).

The Law of 36

2   15   22   30   31   48

2, 22 and 48 gives you 36. At this point, please tell me you now know that 48 is 12?

Dream:

You are spending Money (2) on this Mansion (25) because you are expecting a Baby (9). You also want to sell your Car (11) and your Music (20) collection. You smile at that thought so much your Teeth (21) are showing.

Law Of 36

9   11   20   21   25   2

9, 25 and 2 = 36.

Dream:

You are attending a Funeral (26) of A Crooked (43 also 7) Driver Pilot (2) who died (40 also 4) through an Airplane (33) Accident (39 also 3).

Law Of 36

2   33   39   40   43   26

35 is your answer...Perfect! What is 43 again?

Dream:

You are attending a Funeral (26) where a Fat (44 also 8) Priest (30) is preaching. Suddenly a very Drunk (8) Ill-mannered wife (32) starts to sob uncontrollably, saying her King (1) is dead. This had some Young Boy (33) giggling.

Law of 36

26   30   32   33   44   1

35 is what you get when you add the highlighted numbers. 44? Huh? You are getting it now.

The Dream and Numbers:

You see a Gentleman (6) who has quite a fortune (4) who somehow, has married a crooked (7) Lady (17), who sometimes behaves like a whore (15) when drunk (8).

Law Of 36

4   6   7   8   15   17

The highlighted numbers add up to 36.

(Practice on The Law of 36 on your own)

The Dream and Numbers:

You see a Gentleman (6) who has quite a fortune (4) who somehow, has married a crooked (7) Lady (17), who sometimes behaves like a whore (15) when drunk (8).

…You are in a hospital, sitting next to a Pregnant Woman (8), who is telling you that she wants to have a natural child birth. She wants to deliver through her Vagina (35), but since it's her first, it gives her some Butterflies (18), and she says that, showing her Mouth (24) to you but clenches her Teeth (21). You could almost feel her Excitement (31). And later she comes out showing this baby (27).

Dream:

You have this nightmare about this woman with a glossy Lipstick (31), who your husband spend Money (2) and buy her Shoes (22). You later run into her and you call her a Slut (15) and hold her by the Throat (30). You throw her into a Fire (12). Wow, this is scary.

New Yorkers are Dreamers….

You are in a cab, and you talking to an Indian (30) Driver (2), when a Cop (27), stops a cab for speeding. There is an Argument (5) between the two and then they grab each other by their Clothes (16). You abandon the cab and decide to catch a Train (10).

Realistic isn't it? It's like you had this dream yesterday.

2 Philippines Super-Lotto   **9 Nov 2011 Numbers 12 19 21 25 47 49**

The Dream:

You see yourself living large with a Mansion (25) and you are out fishing (21). Your increases and you get this Big Fish (49 also 13). You get into your Car (47 also 11) and drive home and on the driveway, you get a warm welcome form you Little Girl (19) who takes you in the house. Your first sight is this warm glowing Fire (12) in the grand hall. You thank the lord for your blessings and suddenly…you wake up. You have been dreaming:

Mega Dreams for Mega Millions…

You are attending a Funeral (26) where a Fat (44 also 8) Priest (30) is preaching. Suddenly a very Drunk (8) Ill-mannered wife (32) starts to sob uncontrollably, saying her King (1) is dead. This had some Young Boy (33) giggling.

Dream:

...you go to the fridge and open it, and then you take out some Pork (8) Ribs (11) out and put them on a Dish (45 also 9). You try to pull a piece to taste, but decide to use a Small Knife (15). Then you take some Eggs (10) and boil them. You wipe the fat from the ribs with your Handkerchief (20)."

Dream:

You dream you are in Rainy weather (18) fishing (21: a fisherman). You are surprised (28) to catch a Tiger (5) shark. When you cut open it with a small knife (15), you see it had some Eggs (10) about to leave its body.

Dream:

...you are lured by the charm of this Gentleman (6) and lady (17) who promises you Money (2). They invite you to their House (23) and you go with a smile on your face. On arrival, you notice the house is huge but very Hollow (35). You notice there's Blood (01) on the floor and you run out of the house.

ALL RESULTS COURTESY OF *THE LOTTER.COM*

Online Resources

We have posted a number of posts, using the results of the most recent International using most of major sites around the world.

We also publish the site Stats, showing the growth and support of all the viewers as they visit our site.

We also have a Facebook page where people do inbox us a lot for personal dream interpretations sessions.

Visit: http://mydreamismykey.blogspot.com

Join us on Facebook: My Dream **Is** My Key.

We also do partake in most of the affiliated site where Dreams are discussed.

Disclaimer

The work of the author and his advisors on Fa-Fi are NOT a guarantee that you shall win lottery, Power-ball or any game of chance.

The work clearly intends to show you how to convert the dream symbols into lucky numbers for lotto, power-ball and any other game of chance.

We hope your Dreams Help You Win the Fortune as your heart desires.
GOOD LUCK YOU ALL!

www.ingramcontent.com/pod-product-compliance
Lightning Source LLC
Chambersburg PA
CBHW041524280526
45792CB00004B/1372